The Lady Who Spoke the Qur'ān

By
Shaykh Mufti Saiful Islām

JKN Publications

© Copyright by JKN Publications

First Published in December 2018

ISBN: 978-1-909114-36-4

British Library Cataloguing in Publication Data
A catalogue record for this book is available from the British Library.

All Rights Reserved. No part of this book may be reproduced, stored in a retrieval system or transmitted in any form or by any means, electronic, mechanical, photocopying, recording or otherwise, without the prior permission of the copyright owner.

Publisher's Note:

Every care and attention has been put into the production of this book. If however you find any errors, they are own, for which we seek Allāh's ﷻ forgiveness and reader's pardon.

Published by:

JKN Publications
118 Manningham Lane
Bradford
West Yorkshire
BD8 7JF
United Kingdom

t: +44 (0) 1274 308 456 | w: www.jkn.org.uk | e: info@jkn.org.uk

Book Title: The Lady Who Spoke The Qur'ān

Author: Shaykh Mufti Saiful Islām

Printed by Mega Printing in Turkey

"In the Name of Allāh, the Most Beneficent, the Most Merciful"

Content

Introduction	5
Purpose of Creation	7
Blessings of Allāh ﷻ	8
Life of this World	10
Importance of Time	11
Safeguarding the Tongue	12
Observing Silence	13
An Inspirational Incident – The Lady Who Spoke The Qur'ān	14
Preparation for the Hereafter	23
The Holy Prophet ﷺ - A Perfect Role Model	25
Muāsharāt - An Essential Part of Dīn	26
Five Signs Before the Day of Judgement	27
Islamic Greeting	27
History of Salām	28
As-Salām is an Attribute of Allāh ﷻ	29
Reality of the Islamic Greeting	29
Virtues of Salām	30
Best Act in Islām	31
Our Condition Today	32
The Practice of the Noble Companions ﷺ	33
Frequent Salām	34
Act of Charity	35
Salām to Children	36
Salām When Entering the Home	37
Ādāb of Salām	38
Perfect Role Model	39
Should I Forsake the Sunnah for the Sake of these Fools?	40

Introduction

All praises be to Allāh ﷻ, the Most Beneficent, the Most Merciful and may peace and blessings be sent upon the Beloved Prophet, Guide and Final Messenger, Muhammad ﷺ, upon his beloved family and Companions ؓ.

An important requirement for a Muslim's life is to be careful about time, invest it wisely and benefit from it. Islām encourages Muslims to take care of their time, to utilise it and not to waste it. Besides, it holds them responsible for their time. There is a popular saying "Time is Gold". However, time in Islām is more than gold in this world. Of all the religions, only Islām guides mankind not only to the importance of time but also how to value it. Allāh ﷻ and His Messenger ﷺ very clearly tell us the value of time, why we must not waste it and how we can make use of our time wisely to increase our Imān (Faith) and thus attain success, especially eternal success in the life Hereafter. My beloved Shaykh has mentioned in his book, 'Hadīth for Beginners,' a beautiful Hadīth narrated by Sayyidunā Abdullāh Ibn Abbās ؓ that the Holy Prophet ﷺ said,

"There are two blessings regarding which the majority of people are unaware of i.e. health and free time." (Bukhāri)

Indeed, we displease Allāh ﷻ the Most High when we abuse time. We must remember that time must be spent to fulfil our very purpose in life that is to worship Allāh ﷻ throughout our lives. Allāh ﷻ makes this very clear in the Holy Qur'ān when He says that He only created Jinn and mankind so that they may worship Him. We must understand that time is the measure of life, time is an Amānah (trust), time is a gift from the Creator and its proper use will determine our outcome for eternity.

The Holy Prophet ﷺ was sent as a role model who was the physical form of the Holy Qur'ān. Following the ways of the Holy Prophet ﷺ in every second of our lives is pivotal for success. This booklet tells us the way to gain this success. It also includes an inspirational incident of an amazing lady who only spoke from the Holy Qur'an throughout her life. We will leave it to our readers to marvel at her intelligence, knowledge and piety expressed in this breath-taking episode. May Allāh ﷻ benefit us all from this booklet and facilitate our understanding in this matter. Āmīn!

Maulāna Ismāīl Azīz
Graduate, Jāmiah Khātamun Nabiyeen
December 2018

Purpose of Creation

Allāh ﷻ has created us for a test, a trial. Allāh ﷻ, the Creator of the heavens and the earth has explained this very clearly in His Holy Book. He mentions in a particular verse:

$$\text{وَيَسْتَخْلِفَكُمْ فِي الْأَرْضِ فَيَنظُرَ كَيْفَ تَعْمَلُونَ}$$

"He will make you successors on the earth so that He may see how you act." (7:129)

In Sūrah Al-Mulk, verse 2, Allāh ﷻ states:

$$\text{الَّذِي خَلَقَ الْمَوْتَ وَالْحَيَاةَ لِيَبْلُوَكُمْ أَيُّكُمْ أَحْسَنُ عَمَلًا}$$

"He has created death and life, so that He may test you, which of you is best in deed." (67:02)

In Sūrah Az-Zāriyāth, verse 56, He categorically says:

$$\text{وَمَا خَلَقْتُ الْجِنَّ وَالْإِنسَ إِلَّا لِيَعْبُدُونِ}$$

"And I (Allāh) created not the Jinns and men except they should worship Me (alone)." (51:56)

He has created us for Him and He has created the whole of the universe for us. Allāh ﷻ says:

$$\text{هُوَ الَّذِي خَلَقَ لَكُم مَّا فِي الْأَرْضِ جَمِيعًا}$$

"It is He, Who created for you all that is on earth." (2:29)

Subḥān-Allāh, how Merciful is Allāh ﷻ, how Generous is Allāh ﷻ and how Gracious is Allāh ﷻ? But what does mankind do in return for all His unlimited and infinite favours?

Blessings of Allāh ﷻ

وَإِن تَعُدُّوا نِعْمَةَ اللَّهِ لَا تُحْصُوهَا

"If you try to enumerate the blessings of Allāh, you will not be able to count them." (14:34)

Allāh ﷻ reminds mankind that remember Me as your Creator. Do not renegade and do not rebel against Me.

كَيْفَ تَكْفُرُونَ بِاللَّهِ وَكُنتُمْ أَمْوَاتًا

"How can you disbelieve in Allāh, seeing that you were dead." (2:28)

فَأَحْيَاكُمْ ثُمَّ يُمِيتُكُمْ ثُمَّ يُحْيِيكُمْ ثُمَّ إِلَيْهِ تُرْجَعُونَ

"And He gave you life, then He will give you death, then again will bring you to life (on the Day of Judgement) and then unto Him you will return." (2:28)

How ungrateful is man that he expresses his arrogance and ingratitude towards his Merciful Creator. Allāh ﷻ is so Merciful, so Kind, Subḥān-Allāh, in one verse He says addressing us:

مَّا يَفْعَلُ اللَّهُ بِعَذَابِكُمْ إِن شَكَرْتُمْ وَآمَنتُمْ ۚ وَكَانَ اللَّهُ شَاكِرًا عَلِيمًا

"O' People, why should Allāh punish you if you have thanked

Him and believed in Him. And Allāh is Ever All-Appreciative (of good) All Knowing." (4:147)

Allāh ﷻ has made mankind the best of all His creation. In Sūrah At-Tīn, He says:

$$لَقَدْ خَلَقْنَا الْإِنْسَانَ فِي أَحْسَنِ تَقْوِيْمٍ$$

"Verily, We created man of the best stature (mould)." (95:04)

If Allāh ﷻ has created us for a meaningful purpose, then we have to fulfil this purpose. We cannot pass our time in useless and futile pursuits.

$$أَيَحْسَبُ الْإِنْسَانُ أَنْ يُتْرَكَ سُدًى$$

"Does man think he will be left neglected (without being punished or rewarded for the obligatory duties enjoined by his Lord on him)." (75:36)

Let us not be like the disbelievers who said:

$$وَقَالُوْا مَا هِيَ إِلَّا حَيَاتُنَا الدُّنْيَا نَمُوْتُ وَنَحْيَا وَمَا يُهْلِكُنَا إِلَّا الدَّهْرُ$$

"And they say: There is nothing but our life of this world, we die and we live and nothing destroys us except Ad-Dahr (time)." (45:24)

Life of this World

We have to realise that we have to fulfil our obligation for which we have been sent to this world. If we fail to comply then we have no abode other than Hell. The Holy Prophet ﷺ has said:

اَلدُّنْيَا سِجْنُ الْمُؤْمِنِ وَجَنَّةُ الْكَافِرِ

> "The world is a prison for the believer and paradise for a disbeliever." (Muslim, Tirmizi)

In other words, the Holy Prophet ﷺ has compared the life of a believer to the life of a prison, because a person who is inside a prison does not have the freedom to do what he wishes, he does not have access to all the luxuries, delicacies and amusements of the outside world. In the same way a Mu'min, a believer has to comply and abide by the orders and commands of Allāh ﷻ, thus restrict oneself from the so called amusements, luxuries and delicacies of this world.

On the contrary, a disbeliever who denies Allāh ﷻ enjoys the pleasure of this world the way he pleases. He follows his carnal desires and never stops to think about the ultimate result and consequence of this pleasure. He has actually made his own lust as his god. How beautifully Allāh ﷻ illustrates this point. He states in Sūrah Al-Jāthiyah, verse 23:

اَفَرَاَيْتَ مَنِ اتَّخَذَ اِلٰهَهُ هَوٰهُ

> "Have you seen him who takes his own lust (vain desires) as his Ilāh (God)." (45:23)

He fulfils his lust and desires all the time and whatever is aroused in him, he does. In Tafsīr Rāzi it says:

اَلدُّنْيَا مَزْرَعَةُ الْاخِرَةِ

"This world is a plantation of the Hereafter."

If we plant our seeds of good deeds in this world, we will reap the fruits of the Hereafter, but if we fail to do so, we will be empty-handed. No miracles will take place. Let us make a firm resolution that we will spend every second of our life, which was bestowed to us by our Creator, according to His pleasure, not the pleasure of our Nafs.

Importance of Time

Time is very precious, every second is valuable. When Allāh ﷻ explains the importance of time, He takes an oath on time.

وَالْعَصْرِ إِنَّ الْإِنْسَانَ لَفِيْ خُسْرٍ

"By the oath of time. Verily man is at loss" (103:1-2)

Why is he at loss? It is because he is destroying his time, his life and his assets. If time elapses, it will never come back. Worldly gains, if once lost or missed, could be regained or recovered, but no one on the surface of the earth could bring back a second which he had misused. We have not valued time like the way it should be valued. To actually realise the value of one year, ask the student who failed by a grade. To realise the value of one month, ask the mother who gave birth to a premature baby. To realise the value of one day, ask the editor of a daily newspaper. To realise the value of one hour, ask the bride waiting to be wed. To realise the value of one minute, ask the man who just missed the train. To realise the value of one second, ask the person who just avoided an accident. To realise the value of one millisecond, ask the Olympian who qualified for the bronze.

Today if we ask ourselves what is the most valuable thing we are destroying with our own hands, we will come to the conclusion that it is the invaluable gift of time. We have 1,440 minutes everyday at our disposal. But these valuable minutes are spent in idle pursuits. We occupy and engross ourselves in backbiting, slandering, swearing and committing sins.

Safeguarding the Tongue

The Holy Prophet ﷺ has said,

مَنْ يَّضْمَنْ لِيْ مَا بَيْنَ لِحْيَيْهِ وَمَا بَيْنَ فَخِذَيْهِ اَضْمَنْ لَهُ الْجَنَّةَ

"Whoever guarantees for me (the correct use of) that which is between his jaws (i.e. tongue) and that which is between his thighs (i.e. private parts), I guarantee him paradise." (Bukhārī)

Most sins are committed by the tongue and the private parts. Since the tongue commits more sins than the private parts, the Holy Prophet ﷺ has mentioned the tongue before the private parts. This is also clear from the Hadīth of Bukhārī and Muslim narrated by Sayyidunā Abdullāh Ibn Amr ؓ and Sayyidunā Jābir ؓ;

$$\text{اَلْمُسْلِمُ مَنْ سَلِمَ الْمُسْلِمُوْنَ مِنْ لِسَانِهِ وَيَدِهِ}$$

"A true believer is he from whose mouth and hand other believers stay safe." (Bukhāri, Muslim)

The Holy Prophet ﷺ has mentioned the tongue first, then the hand. We must safeguard our tongue from all kinds of evil. A large amount of people will be entering the Hell-Fire due to the tongue. Think about it! This same tongue, can be used to proclaim faith and enter the fold of Islām, which will bring eternal bliss. On the contrary if one utters the words of disbelief, he will throw himself eternally into the blazing Hell-Fire.

Observing Silence

We should observe silence and only talk when it is necessary. The Hadīth narrated by Imām Tirmizi ؓ from Sayyidunā Abdullāh Ibn Amr ؓ says,

$$\text{مَنْ صَمَتَ نَجَا}$$

"He who keeps silent saves himself." (Tirmizi)

Imām Bukhāri ؓ narrates a Hadīth from Sayyidunā Abū Hurairah ؓ that the Holy Prophet ﷺ said,

$$\text{مَنْ كَانَ يُؤْمِنُ بِاللهِ وَالْيَوْمِ الْاٰخِرِ فَلْيَقُلْ خَيْرًا اَوْ لِيَصْمُتْ}$$

"Whoever has faith in Allāh and the Last Day should either speak what is good or remain silent." (Bukhāri, Muslim)

A person who safeguards his tongue, is less likely to commit errors and faults. Thus, the Holy Prophet ﷺ says,

مَنْ خَزَنَ لِسَانَهُ سَتَرَ اللهُ عَوْرَتَهُ

"Whoever guards his tongue, Allāh ﷻ will conceal his faults." (Baihaqi)

Allāh ﷻ in Sūrah Qāf, verse 18, proclaims,

مَا يَلْفِظُ مِن قَوْلٍ إِلَّا لَدَيْهِ رَقِيبٌ عَتِيدٌ

"He utters no word but there is with him an observer ready (to record it)." (50:18)

كِرَامًا كَاتِبِينَ يَعْلَمُونَ مَا تَفْعَلُونَ

"The Kirāman Kātibīn they know (all) that you do." (82:11-12)

Every word uttered is written by the two angels appointed with every person. The angel on the right shoulder records the good deeds whilst the angel on the left shoulder records the bad deeds.

An Inspirational Incident

Our pious predecessors restrained and safeguarded their tongues from not only useless talk but even permissible talk lest they fall into sins. I would like to share with you an incident, which is so inspiring and amazing that it makes us realise the importance of safeguarding the tongue.

The Lady Who Spoke The Qur'ān — An Inspirational Incident

Once Imām Abū Hanīfah's ﷺ student, Abdullāh Ibn Mubārak ﷺ, was travelling from Makkah to Madīnah, when he came across a woman in the midst of a desert. What happened next is for all to remember. The scholars have concluded that the knowledgeable woman was either Rābiya Basri or Umme Yahyā.

Note: Every sentence said by Rābiya Basri is from the Holy Qur'ān.

Abdullāh:

اَلسَّلَامُ عَلَيْكُمْ وَرَحْمَةُ اللهِ وَبَرَكَاتُهُ

Rābiya:

سَلَامٌ قَوْلًا مِّن رَّبٍّ رَّحِيْمٍ

"A word from a Merciful Lord is Peace." (36:58)

Abdullāh: "May Allāh's ﷻ blessing be upon you! What are you doing here?"

Rābiya:

مَنْ يُّضْلِلِ اللهُ فَلَا هَادِيَ لَهُ

"Those whom Allāh sends astray, there is no guide for them." (7:186)

Abdullāh [thinking she has lost her way]: "In which direction are you travelling?"

Rābiya:

سُبْحَانَ الَّذِيْ أَسْرَىٰ بِعَبْدِهِ لَيْلًا مِّنَ الْمَسْجِدِ الْحَرَامِ إِلَى الْمَسْجِدِ الْأَقْصَى

"Glory to (Allāh) Who carried His servant by night from Masjid-ul-Harām to the far distant place of worship (Masjid-ul-Aqsā)." (17:01)

Abdullāh [concluding that people returning from Hajj travel to Baitul-Maqdis]: "For how long have you remained here?"

Rābiya:

ثَلَاثَ لَيَالٍ سَوِيًّا

"For three whole nights." (19:10)

Abdullāh [astonished]: "But how have you been surviving when you have no food or drink?"

Rābiya:

وَالَّذِيْ هُوَ يُطْعِمُنِيْ وَيَسْقِيْنِ

"He is that Being Who feeds me and gives me drink." (26:79)

Abdullāh: "But if you have no water, how have you been making ablution?"

Rābiya:

فَلَمْ تَجِدُوْا مَاءً فَتَيَمَّمُوْا صَعِيْدًا طَيِّبًا

"And if you find no water then take for yourselves clean earth." (4:43)

Abdullāh: "I have food with me! Would you like to eat now?"

Rābiya:

ثُمَّ أَتِمُّوا الصِّيَامَ إِلَى اللَّيْلِ

"Complete your fast till night." (2:187)

Abdullāh: "But why are you fasting? When surely this is not the month of Ramadhān."

Rābiya:

وَمَن تَطَوَّعَ خَيْرًا فَإِنَّ اللَّهَ شَاكِرٌ عَلِيمٌ

"He who does good with his own free will; it is better for him. For surely Allāh is the Most Grateful and the All Knowing." (2:158)

Abdullāh: "However, it has been excused for Muslims not to fast whilst travelling."

Rābiya:

وَأَن تَصُومُوا خَيْرٌ لَّكُمْ إِن كُنتُمْ تَعْلَمُونَ

"And if you fast it is better for you if only you know." (2:184)

Abdullāh [in frustration]: "Why do you speak Qur'anic verses only? Why do you not speak in my language?"

Rābiya:

مَا يَلْفِظُ مِن قَوْلٍ إِلَّا لَدَيْهِ رَقِيبٌ عَتِيدٌ

"He utters no word but there is with him an observer." (50:18)
[meaning the angels who take account of our deeds]

Abdullāh: "Which tribe do you come from?"

Rābiya:

$$\text{وَلَا تَقْفُ مَا لَيْسَ لَكَ بِهِ عِلْمٌ}$$

"And follow not that of which you have no knowledge." (17:36)

Abdullāh [ashamed, pleadingly]: "Please forgive me, yet again I have been proven wrong."

Rābiya [forgivably]:

$$\text{لَا تَثْرِيبَ عَلَيْكُمُ الْيَوْمَ}$$

"There shall be no blame on you today." (12:92)

Abdullāh: "Come ride upon my camel and I shall take you safely to your destination."

Rābiyah:

$$\text{وَمَا تَفْعَلُوا مِنْ خَيْرٍ يَعْلَمْهُ اللّٰهُ}$$

"And whatsoever good you do, Allāh knows." (2:197)

Having reared the camel to crouch down, Abdullāh Ibn Mubārak ﷺ then indicated Rābiya to mount onto the camel.

Rābiya:

$$\text{قُلْ لِلْمُؤْمِنِينَ يَغُضُّوا مِنْ أَبْصَارِهِمْ وَيَحْفَظُوا فُرُوجَهُمْ}$$

"Say to the believing men that they should lower their gaze and be modest." (24:30)

After lowering the gaze, Abdullāh Ibn Mubārak ﷺ told Rābiya to mount upon the camel.

Just as she began to mount on, the camel moved forward which caused her shawl to fall slightly to which she said:

فَبِمَا كَسَبَتْ أَيْدِيكُمْ

"It is because of the things your hands have earned." (42:30)

Abdullāh: "Wait, let me first tie the camel down so that it may remain still for you to mount upon it."

Rābiya:

فَفَهَّمْنَاهَا سُلَيْمَانَ

"And We have made Sulaimān understand (the case)." (21:79)

After tying the camel down once again, Abdullāh Ibn Mubārak ﷺ told Rābiya to mount upon the camel. Whilst mounting, she began to praise Allāh ﷻ.

Rābiya:

سُبْحَانَ الَّذِي سَخَّرَ لَنَا هَٰذَا وَمَا كُنَّا لَهُ مُقْرِنِينَ

"Glory be to Him Who has subjected this for our use for we could never have accomplished this (by ourselves)." (43:13)

Abdullāh Ibn Mubārak ﷺ whilst holding onto the rope of the camel began praying loudly and quickly. Seeing this, Rābiya once again stated another verse.

Rābiya:

وَاقْصِدْ فِي مَشْيِكَ وَاغْضُضْ مِنْ صَوْتِكَ

"And be moderate in your pace and lower your voice." (31:19)

Abdullāh Ibn Mubārak ﷺ: "Allāh ﷻ has granted you with many rewards."

Rābiya:

وَمَا يَذَّكَّرُ إِلَّا أُولُو الْأَلْبَابِ

"But none will grasp the message apart from men of understanding." (3:7)

Abdullāh: "Do you have a companion, a husband?"

Rābiya:

يَا أَيُّهَا الَّذِينَ آمَنُوا لَا تَسْأَلُوا عَنْ أَشْيَاءَ إِنْ تُبْدَ لَكُمْ تَسُؤْكُمْ

"O you who believe, ask not questions about such things that if made clear to you, may cause you trouble." (5:101)

After hearing this, Abdullāh Ibn Mubārak ﷺ remained silent until he approached a group of people. Abdullāh [upon arrival] said, "What family do you have amongst this tribe?"

Rābiya:

الْمَالُ وَالْبَنُونَ زِينَةُ الْحَيَاةِ الدُّنْيَا

"Wealth and sons are an ornament of the life of this world." (18:46)

Abdullāh Ibn Mubārak ﷺ realised that she had sons within the tribe. He then asked for her address.
Rābiya:

وَعَلَامَاتٍ وَبِالنَّجْمِ هُمْ يَهْتَدُونَ

"And marks and signposts and by the stars (men) guide themselves." (16:16)

Abdullāh Ibn Mubārak ﷺ held on to the lead of the camel and began to circulate amongst the tents asking whether she recognised her tent.

When passing one particular tent, Rābiya called out the following verses:

وَاتَّخَذَ اللهُ إِبْرَاهِيمَ خَلِيلًا

"And Allāh made Ibrāheem a close friend." (4:125)

وَكَلَّمَ اللهُ مُوسَىٰ تَكْلِيمًا

"And Allāh spoke directly to Mūsā." (4:164)

يَا يَحْيَىٰ خُذِ الْكِتَابَ بِقُوَّةٍ

"O' Yahyā hold fast onto the scripture." (19:12)

Abdullāh Ibn Mubārak ﷺ now knew that she had three sons, Mūsā, Yahyā and Ibrāhīm, so raising his voice, he began to call for the three. No sooner had the words left his mouth that three handsome young men came running upon hearing their names being called out. Seeing their mother, they lowered her from the camel and began a conversation with Abdullāh Ibn Mubārak ﷺ.

Rābiya:

$$\text{فَابْعَثُوا أَحَدَكُم بِوَرِقِكُمْ هَٰذِهِ إِلَى الْمَدِينَةِ فَلْيَنظُرْ أَيُّهَا أَزْكَىٰ طَعَامًا فَلْيَأْتِكُم بِرِزْقٍ مِّنْهُ}}$$

"Now send one of you with this silver coin into the city, and let him see what food is purest there and bring a supply thereof." (18:19)

Immediately hearing this, one son hurried away, only to return with some food which he put in front of Abdullāh Ibn Mubārak ﷺ.

Rābiya:

$$\text{كُلُوا وَاشْرَبُوا هَنِيئًا بِمَا أَسْلَفْتُمْ فِي الْأَيَّامِ الْخَالِيَةِ}}$$

"Eat and drink with ease for that which you carried out in the days past." (69:24)

Abdullāh Ibn Mubārak ﷺ became fully aware of Rābiya's ﷺ piety and great ability in understanding the Holy Qur'ān. From the beginning to the end of the journey, she had answered from the Holy Qur'ān, not once speaking her own language.

He cried out in panic to her sons, "I swear not to touch this food until I have been told who this pious woman is!"

Astonished by Abdullāh Ibn Mubārak's ﷺ outcry, her sons answered, "We have no reason not to tell you. She is our mother who has for the last forty years only spoken from the Holy Qur'ān, using wholly Qur'anic verses, so that on the Day of Judgement, she will not have to answer for any sins committed by her tongue." Subhān-Allāh!

Preparation for the Hereafter

These are our pious predecessors. But today, our life is being destroyed by the internet, TV and mobile phones etc. and at the same time we are deprived of Allāh's mercy. We are committing sins 24 hours around the clock and at the same time when someone advices us to stop committing sins, we rudely reply, "Allāh is Gafoor, He is very Forgiving; He will forgive our sins." This is complete foolishness and stupidity.

The Hadīth of the Holy Prophet says,

اَلْكَيِّسُ مَنْ دَانَ نَفْسَهُ وَعَمِلَ لِمَا بَعْدَ الْمَوْتِ وَالْعَاجِزُ مَنْ اَتْبَعَ نَفْسَهُ هَوَاهَا وَتَمَنَّى عَلَى اللهِ

"The intelligent person is the one who suppresses his Nafs and works for the life after death and the foolish person is the one who follows his desires and depends on Allāh." (Tirmizi, Ibn Mājah)

Let us make a firm resolution to change our lives today, repent from all sins. The Holy Prophet said,

اَلتَّائِبُ مِنَ الذَّنْبِ كَمَنْ لاَ ذَنْبَ لَهُ

"The repenter from sins is like the one who has no sins."
(Ibn Mājah, Tabarāni)

Let us value our time. The beautiful Hadīth of the Holy Prophet ﷺ narrated by Imām Tirmizi ﷜, speaks volumes on the importance of time.

اِغْتَنِمْ خَمْسًا قَبْلَ خَمْسٍ شَبَابَكَ قَبْلَ هَرَمِكَ وَصِحَّتَكَ قَبْلَ سَقَمِكَ وَغِنَاكَ قَبْلَ فَقْرِكَ وَفَرَاغَكَ قَبْلَ شُغْلِكَ وَحَيُوتَكَ قَبْلَ مَوْتِكَ

"Treasure five things before five:
1. Your youth before your old age.
2. Your health before your illness.
3. Your prosperity before your poverty.
4. Your free time before your engagement.
5. Your life before your death." (Tirmizi)

May Allāh ﷻ bestow us the strength and ability to act upon Islām and make us understand the true value of time. Āmīn!

Salām - Islamic Greeting

The Holy Prophet ﷺ - A Perfect Role Model

Islamic lifestyle has no parallel. Islām provides moral guidelines to every aspect of human life and gives the solution to our daily problematic issues. The Holy Prophet ﷺ is an exemplary role model for the whole of mankind. So the question arises: Why is there any need for Muslims to emulate the conduct of others?

Amongst the Islamic teachings is the inculcating of humility, sympathy and unity in order to attain stability in our lives. Consider for example, the Islamic conduct pertaining to eating and drinking. The Holy Prophet ﷺ demonstrated this conduct verbally as well as practically.

He said, "I eat as a slave eats." It was the noble character of our beloved Prophet ﷺ to eat whilst sitting in a humble position with his body inclined towards the food. He would eat quickly with appreciation.

In contrast, we eat with great pride and with style. There is no sign of humility in us when we eat. Such arrogant conduct is the result of the reality of life being hidden from us. Once the reality becomes revealed to a person, he will realise that whatever he is eating is from the Court of the King of kings (Allāh ﷻ) and that He is observing every action that we do.

Thus automatically, the humble manner of the Holy Prophet ﷺ will be adopted. When the greatness of a Supreme Being is rooted in the heart then all stages will be traversed with ease.

The fact is that we lack the ability to realise that Allāh ﷻ is watching us. Now, when Islām possesses its code of conduct in a state of perfection, then what need do Muslims have to emulate others?

Honour, self-respect and our claim of the perfection of our Dīn demands that we strictly adhere to its teachings entirely and to the moral code of conduct ordained by Allāh ﷻ and the Holy Prophet ﷺ.

Muāsharāt (Social Conduct) - An Essential Part of Dīn

We must endeavour to adopt the beautiful teachings of Islām in every aspect of our lives. Reformation of Muāsharāt is imperative since it is an essential branch of Dīn. Just as Salāh and Sawm are compulsory, so too is Muāsharāt. Nowadays people not only consider Muāsharāt as insignificant but also no longer view it as an integral aspect of Dīn. In fact, all the books of Ahādīth consist of chapters pertaining to Muāsharāt. The scholars of the past have elaborated on this spectrum of life. But unfortunately, no one is prepared to pay any heed to this vital branch of Islām.

The Ādāb (etiquettes) of Muāsharāt are continuously diminishing by the day even though they are common sense. Our beautiful Islamic teachings are daily being disregarded by the Muslims themselves. This surely is an indication that the Day of Qiyāmah is very close.

Five Signs Before the Day of Judgement

Sayyidunā Abdullāh Ibn Mas'ūd ﷺ relates that our beloved Prophet ﷺ said, "Before the Day of Qiyāmah, from amongst the many signs to come will be:

1. The offering of Salām will be confined to acquaintances.
2. Businesses will expand to the extent that the wives will begin to assist their husbands to conduct trade.
3. Family relations will be severed.
4. Those giving false testimony will become heroes, and true testimony will be suppressed.
5. The competent and the incompetent will begin to write books." (Ahmad)

Sadly, the aforementioned signs are rampant amongst the Muslims today. I would like to merely touch on the first sign mentioned in this Hadīth of Musnad Ahmad.

Islamic Greeting

The Hadīth states that offering Salām will be confined to acquaintances only. This is precisely what is happening in our society today. We must adopt the correct teachings and methods concerning this matter.

We know that every civilised community on earth has a particular mode of greeting which is expressed when members of the community meet. These words of salutation are to express friendship and courtesy. None of these phrases compare with the greeting of Islām, which is not only a greeting, but also a Du'ā (supplication).

Before the advent of Islām, the Arabs greeted one another with such phrases as حَيَّاكَ الله (may Allāh ﷻ grant you life) or أَنْعِم صَبَاحاً (may you be blessed this morning). In today's society, "hello", "good morning", "good afternoon" and "good-bye" etc. are used to exchange greetings.

History of Salām

Allāh ﷻ replaced all modern methods of greeting with the best greeting which was used by all the noble Prophets ﷺ. He has commanded the progeny of Sayyidunā Ādam ﷺ that they greet each other with the salutation of Salām (peace) which is in fact a Du'ā. Sayyidunā Abū Hurairah ؓ relates that the Holy Prophet ﷺ said, "Allāh ﷻ created Ādam ﷺ and his height was sixty arms length. Allāh ﷻ said to him, 'Go and offer Salām (salutations of peace) to them (a group of angels who were seated) and listen to their reply for that will be your greeting and the greeting of your progeny.' So he said to them 'As-Salāmu-Alaikum (peace be upon you).' They replied, 'Wa-Alaikumus-Salām Wa Rahmatullāh (may peace and mercy of Allāh ﷻ be upon you).' They added, 'Wa Rahmatullāh' (and the mercy of Allāh ﷻ). Whosoever will enter Jannah (Paradise) will be according to his (Ādam ﷺ) height and He

(Allāh ﷻ) had reduced the height of His creation up to this time (the period of the beloved Prophet ﷺ). (Bukhāri, Muslim)

As-Salām is an Attribute of Allāh ﷻ

According to one Hadīth, Sayyidunā Abdullāh Ibn Mas'ūd ؓ relates that the Holy Prophet ﷺ said, "Salām is from the attributes of Allāh ﷻ which He has placed on earth. Therefore, make Salām (greeting) common amongst you."(Adabul-Mufrad)

Reality of the Islamic Greeting

The Islamic greeting (Salām) is an inclusive term and it is also a Du'ā which encompasses all that which brings about peace and good fortune to a Muslim's life. Whilst a Muslim is wishing his fellow Muslim brother peace, he is simultaneously praying for his protection from all misfortunes, calamities etc.

Therefore, Islām has modified the pre-Islamic and modern methods of greeting to As-Salāmu-Alaikum, which means (may peace be upon you i.e. may you be free from all difficulty, calamity and anxiety). The Islamic greeting not only illustrates an example of friendship and respect but also fulfils the rights of a Muslim in the form of a Du'ā. When greeting a Muslim we are beseeching Allāh ﷻ to save that person from all calamites and worries.

The Salām is not only a brief Du'ā i.e. 'may you live long;' it is more comprehensive i.e. 'may you also have a prosperous and protected life'. It also reminds the Muslims to whom it is expressed, that both of us are in need of Allāh ﷻ. We cannot benefit nor harm one another without Allāh's ﷻ will. The greeting of Salām is regarded as an act of Ibādah (act of worship) because it is uttered in compliance with the teachings of our beloved Prophet ﷺ. By correctly understanding the reality of the Islamic greeting and making it a universal mode of greeting, we can make it the means of resolving many of the problems facing Muslims. That is why our beloved Prophet ﷺ has strongly exhorted us to make the Salām frequent amongst ourselves.

Virtues of Salām

Allāh ﷻ has instructed us to greet our Muslim brothers and sisters. Allāh ﷻ states in the Holy Qur'ān,

وَإِذَا حُيِّيْتُمْ بِتَحِيَّةٍ فَحَيُّوْا بِأَحْسَنَ مِنْهَا أَوْ رُدُّوْهَا

"When you are greeted with a greeting, then reply with a better greeting or return the same greeting." (4:86)

This verse instructs us to greet our fellow Muslims with Salām. It is Sunnah to offer Salām but to reply to Salām is Wājib (compulsory). Sayyidunā Imrān Ibn Husain ؓ relates, "A man came to the Holy Prophet ﷺ and said, 'As-Salāmu Alaikum,' the Holy Prophet ﷺ replied to him and the man sat down. The Holy Prophet ﷺ then said, "Ten," (meaning for him are ten rewards).

"Thereafter another man came and said, 'As-Salāmu Alaikum wa

Rahmatullāh'. The Holy Prophet ﷺ replied to him and the man sat down. The Holy Prophet ﷺ said, "Twenty," (his reward will be twenty).

"Thereafter, another man came and said, 'As-Salāmu Alaikum wa Rahmatullāhi wa Barakātuh'. The Holy Prophet ﷺ responded to the man and he sat down. The Holy Prophet ﷺ said, "Thirty," (his reward will be thirty). (Tirmizi, Abū Dāwūd)

In another similar Hadīth, Sayyidunā Ali ؓ relates that the Holy Prophet ﷺ added, "Thirty for you, O' Ali, you and I are equal in Salām. Whosoever passes by a gathering and he greets them with Salām, for him is recorded ten rewards and ten of his sins are forgiven, and he will be raised ten stages in rank."(Ibnus Sunni)

Just ponder over the tremendous rewards for offering Salām and replying to Salām. Salām is the best greeting for wishing peace and tranquillity. We should offer Salām to all Muslims, irrespective of whether they are acquaintances or strangers.

Best Act in Islām

Sayyidunā Abdullāh Ibn Amr Ibn Ās ؓ relates that a man asked the Holy Prophet ﷺ, "What act is the best in Islām?" He replied, "To feed people, (for gaining reward) and to greet people with Salām, those who you know and those who you don't know." (Bukhāri, Muslim)

As I have quoted the Hadīth of Sayyidunā Abdullāh Ibn Mas'ūd ؓ earlier that from amongst the signs of Qiyāmah, is a person who will only offer Salām to his acquaintances, not because of Muslim brotherhood. (Musnad Ahmad)

Sayyidunā Abū Hurairah ؓ reports that the Holy Prophet ﷺ said, "You will not enter Paradise until you become true believers, and you will not become true believers until you love one another. Should I not inform you that which will instil love in one another? To spread Salām amongst you." (Muslim)

In a Hadīth narrated by Sayyidunā Abdullāh Ibn Salām ؓ it is mentioned that the Holy Prophet ﷺ said, "O people! Make Salām common amongst you, provide (people) with food, maintain the ties of kinship, perform Salāh (Tahajjud) when people are asleep, (in return) you will enter Jannah with peace." (Tirmizi)

Our Condition Today

Today Salām is ignored in our lives. We now live in a time where blood relatives cannot stand the sight of one another. To the extent Muslims have severed relationships with close and beloved ones. It is unfortunate to see how many Muslim parents and their grown up sons and daughters have severed their ties with each other, not even willing to offer Salām to each other. It is the pride and arrogance in our hearts which has distanced ourselves away from each other – diverting us further away from the true path and understanding of Islām. If one initiates the Salām, the Hadīth gives glad tidings that such a person is immune from pride and he is closer to

Allāh ﷻ.

Sayyidunā Abdullāh Ibn Mas'ūd ﷺ relates that the Holy Prophet ﷺ said, "The one who initiates Salām first is free from pride." (Baihaqi, Mishkāt)

In another Hadīth, Sayyidunā Abū Umāmah ﷺ relates that the Holy Prophet ﷺ said, "Indeed the closest person to Allāh ﷻ is the one who initiates the Salām." (Abū Dawūd)

In today's society, either we entirely neglect to offer Salām, or wait in anticipation for others to initiate the Salām, even then we do not reply to the Salām, which is Wājib (compulsory).

The Practice of the Noble Companions ﷺ

The noble Companions of the Holy Prophet ﷺ acting upon this Hadīth would go out specifically to say Salām to others. One such Companion was Sayyidunā Abdullāh Ibn Umar ﷺ. He would go out to the market place solely for offering Salām to the people. Tufail ﷺ relates, I once came to Sayyidunā Abdullāh Ibn Umar ﷺ who made me follow him to the market, I asked him, "What do you intend to do in the market place? You do not stop to buy nor enquire about the quality or origin of the merchandise. You don't enquire about the prices nor join those sitting in the market?"

He remarked, "Come here and let us talk." Sayyidunā Abdullāh Ibn Umar ﷺ said, "We go there so that we give Salām to whoever we meet." (Muwatta Imām Mālik, Baihaqi)

It is mentioned in another Hadīth related by Tabarāni that whosoever greets twenty Muslim men (or women) collectively or individually in a day and suddenly passes away on that same day, Jannah will become compulsory upon him, and if it be during the night then likewise.

Moreover, it is narrated in another Hadīth, "Whoever offers Salām to ten Muslims, it would be as if he had freed a slave and if he passed away on that day, Jannah will become necessary for him." (Awjazul Masālik - Shaykh Muhammad Zakariyā ﷺ)

Frequent Salām

Our beloved Prophet ﷺ emphasised the offering of Salām to such an extent that Sayyidunā Abū Hurairah ؓ relates that the Holy Prophet ﷺ said, "Whoever meets his brother he should offer Salām. If they are separated by a tree, wall or a stone then they should greet one another upon meeting (again)." (Abū Dāwūd)

Salām also fulfils the right of a Muslim. Sayyidunā Abū Hurairah ؓ relates that the Holy Prophet ﷺ said, "The rights of a Muslim over another are five." They asked, "What are they?" He replied, "When he meets him he greets him (with Salām), when he invites him he accepts it, when he advises him he accepts the advice, when he sneezes and says 'Alhamdulillāh', he should respond by saying 'Yarhamukallāh', when he is ill he visits him and when he dies he accompanies his Janāzah." (Bukhāri, Muslim)

Let us practise this beautiful Sunnah of the Holy Prophet ﷺ with a pleasant countenance. It may seem insignificant in our eyes but in the eyes of Allāh ﷻ, it is virtuous, deserving tremendous reward in return. Our beloved Prophet ﷺ said, "Do not belittle any good deed, though it may be meeting your Muslim brother with a countenance of affection and happiness." (Muslim)

Act of Charity

Sayyidunā Hasan ؓ relates that the Holy Prophet ﷺ said, "It is an act of charity that you greet people while you show affection and happiness." (Ibn Abi Dunyā)

Nowadays, we assume Sadaqah to be merely giving money to charities whereas our beloved Prophet ﷺ is offering us a prescription where we can achieve the reward of charity all the time. We encounter all kinds of people on a daily basis from our close family members and acquaintances to unfamiliar people on the street. Let us inculcate this noble habit of smiling when we meet our Muslim brothers and sisters.

It is recorded in a Hadīth in Tirmizi by Sayyidunā Abū Zarr ؓ, that the Holy Prophet ﷺ said, "For you to smile when meeting a Muslim brother is a (reward of) Sadaqah (charity) and for you to enjoin him to do good and prevent him from doing evil is (also) Sadaqah. When you guide a man who is astray is a Sadaqah, to remove any obstacle, thorn and bone from the road is a Sadaqah for you and to fill water into your Muslim brother's container from your container is also a Sadaqah for you."

It is reported that on one occasion when Sayyidunā Yahyā ﷺ met Sayyidunā Īsā ﷺ he initiated the Salām, he was also replied with Salām. Whenever he met him, he was happy and smiling whilst Sayyidunā Īsā ﷺ was sorrowful as if he resembled a crying person. Sayyidunā Īsā ﷺ said to him, "You smile like a happy person as if you are secure and protected." Sayyidunā Yahyā ﷺ said, "You show much sorrow like a crying person as if you have despaired." Instantly, Allāh ﷻ revealed to Sayyidunā Īsā ﷺ, "The one who smiles is the most dearest to me." (Tirmizi)

Salām to Children

Our beloved Prophet ﷺ demonstrated a perfect example of commencing the Salām to the extent that he would also offer Salām to children. Sayyidunā Anas Ibn Mālik ﷺ once passed by some children and offered Salām to them and said, "The Holy Prophet ﷺ used to do this to them" (Ahmad, Nasai)

In a Hadīth of Abū Dāwūd it is mentioned that the Holy Prophet ﷺ used to offer Salām to children who were playing when he passed them. Moreover, when we converse over the telephone the same rule is also applicable. To initiate the Salām will be an act of Sunnah and if the caller greets the one answering the telephone it will become Wājib for him to reply to the Salām. Even when entering ones home Salām should be offered. Allāh ﷻ says in the Holy Qur'ān,

فَإِذَا دَخَلْتُمْ بُيُوْتًا فَسَلِّمُوْا عَلٰۤى اَنْفُسِكُمْ تَحِيَّةً مِّنْ عِنْدِ اللّٰهِ مُبٰرَكَةً طَيِّبَةً

"When you enter homes, salute your people with the greeting of peace, a greeting from Allāh (which is) full of blessing and purity." (24:61)

Sayyidunā Anas ؓ relates that the Holy Prophet ﷺ said to him, "O' my son! When you enter your home greet with the salutation of peace. It would be a blessing for you and for the members of your family." (Tirmizi)

There are many blessings that descend from Allāh ﷻ when offering Salām to our family members. What better reward can there be for this noble act.

Sayyidunā Abū Umāmah ؓ says that the Holy Prophet ﷺ said, "Three types of people are in Allāh's ﷻ protection. If they live, Allāh ﷻ will be sufficient for them and if they die they will be admitted into Jannah: (1) Whosoever enters his home saying Salām, he is protected by Allāh ﷻ, (2) Whoever goes to the Masjid is in Allāh's ﷻ protection, (3) Whoever goes in the path of Allāh ﷻ is in Allāh's ﷻ protection." (Ibn Hibbān)

Salām When Entering the Home

The procedure of entering the home is that first the Du'ā of entering the home should be recited which is:

اَللّٰهُمَّ اِنِّیْ اَسْئَلُكَ خَیْرَ الْمَوْلَجِ وَ خَیْرَ الْمَخْرَجِ بِسْمِ اللّٰهِ وَلَجْنَا وَبِسْمِ اللّٰهِ خَرَجْنَا وَعَلَی اللّٰهِ رَبِّنَا تَوَكَّلْنَا

"O Allāh I seek from You the best of returning and the best of emerging. We enter with Allāh's Name and leave with Allāh's Name and upon Allāh ﷻ our Sustainer do we depend."

(Abū Dāwūd)

Thereafter, As-Salāmu Alaikum should be said audibly. Let us implement this into our daily lives so that we can attain the blessings and protection from Allāh ﷻ. Unfortunately, today we are so heedless that we fail to offer Salām to our families and vice versa. This sometimes becomes a root problem in the breakages of family ties. In our daily lives, the father or husband will return home with a grumpy face or very exhausted without a smile or Salām. Rather the first demand the husband makes upon entering the home is, "Get my food on the table." The wife will respond with resentment and use harsh words such as, "I am not your slave" or "Who do you think I am?" This will inevitably result in arguments, physical or verbal abuse or even divorce.

Ādāb of Salām

The Holy Prophet ﷺ would occasionally refuse entry to the one who failed to offer Salām. Sayyidunā Kildā ؓ reports that once Sayyidunā Safwān Ibn Umayyah ؓ sent him with milk and a lamb and some cucumbers for the Holy Prophet ﷺ whilst the Holy Prophet ﷺ was at the top of the valley. He says, "When I entered, I did not offer Salām." Thereupon, the Holy Prophet ﷺ said, "Go out, come back, and say As-Salāmu Alaikum, may I enter?"

It is reported in a Hadīth that if Salām upon entering one's residence is neglected, then Shaytān becomes dominant in that home.

Sayyidunā Jābir ؓ relates that the Holy Prophet ﷺ said, "When a person remembers Allāh ﷻ when he enters his home and when he eats, Shaytān says to his party, 'There is no accommodation for the night and neither any supper for you here.' However, if he enters without remembering Allāh ﷻ, then Shaytān says to his group, 'You have secured your night accommodation.' If he fails to mention Allāh's ﷻ name when he begins his meal, then Shaytān says, 'You have secured your night accommodation and supper." (Muslim)

It is common nowadays for people to increasingly complain about the effect of Jinns and black magic whereas we have failed to understand why this is on the increase at an alarming rate. If we adhere to the teachings of our beloved Prophet ﷺ then there will be peace and tranquillity in our homes.

Perfect Role Model

Let us adopt the Sunnah of our beloved Prophet ﷺ in every aspect of our lives. We will then realise and witness its fruits in this life and the Hereafter. Our beloved Prophet ﷺ was an exemplary role model in every aspect of life. If you wish to become a good father, then observe the example of the noble father of Sayyidah Fātimah ؓ. If you want to become a good husband then observe the example of the noble husband of Sayyidah Ā'ishah ؓ and Sayyidah Khadījah ؓ.

If you want to become a good ruler then see the exemplary practice of the Holy Prophet ﷺ as a ruler in Madīnah Munawwarah. Similarly, if you wish to become an excellent worker or trader then refer to the excellent example of the Holy Prophet ﷺ as a shepherd in the hills of Makkah Mukarramah and his trading in Syria. The Holy Prophet ﷺ was a trader, a reformer, a politician, an economist and so on. In every sphere of life we have a role model in the form of the Holy Prophet ﷺ.

Should I Forsake the Sunnah for the Sake of these Fools?

A prime example of love and devotion for the Sunnah of the Holy Prophet ﷺ is the incident of Sayyidunā Huzaifah Ibn Yamān ؓ in the presence of the king of Persia (modern day Iran). Sayyidunā Huzaifah Ibn Yamān ؓ was once beckoned by Kisrā, the king of Persia, to his court for negotiations. When he reached there, the king presented food to him to illustrate his hospitality. Whilst Sayyidunā Huzaifah ؓ was eating, he accidently dropped a morsel on the ground. In this regard, the Holy Prophet ﷺ said, "If a morsel of food drops from one of you then pick it up, remove the dirt and eat it. Do not leave it for the Shaytān."

Sayyidunā Huzaifah ؓ remembering this Hadīth went to pick up the morsel. However, a man sitting next to him attempted to prevent him by saying, "This is a court of one of the world's super powers. If you pick up the morsel and eat it you will lose all your credibility in their eyes. Therefore, do not pick up the morsel, as it is not an appropriate time." Sayyidunā Huzaifah ؓ responded, "Should I forsake the Sunnah of 'my beloved' for the sake of these fools?"

Whether they like it or not, even if they ridicule me, I am not prepared to abandon the Sunnah of the Holy Prophet ﷺ. The question to consider here is: Did they (the Sahābah ؓ) earn respect on account of their deeds and today are we earning respect on this account or not?

They earned respect because on one hand, they picked up a morsel from the ground to consume it merely to follow the Sunnah and on the other hand, they crushed the symbols of pride (the super powers of the world at that time) to dust with great force as the Holy Prophet ﷺ prophesised.

"Once the Kisrā (the title given to the king of Persia) is perished, there will never be another Kisrā ever again."

As a result, the noble Companions ؓ attained success in both worlds and conquered the Persian Empire by following the Sunnah of the Holy Prophet ﷺ.

May Allāh ﷻ grant us all the ability to follow the Sunnah of the Holy Prophet ﷺ in the correct manner. Āmeen!

Other titles from JKN PUBLICATIONS

Your Questions Answered
An outstanding book written by Shaykh Mufti Saiful Islām. A very comprehensive yet simple Fatāwa book and a source of guidance that reaches out to a wider audience i.e. the English speaking Muslims. The reader will benefit from the various answers to questions based on the Laws of Islām relating to the beliefs of Islām, knowledge, Sunnah, pillars of Islām, marriage, divorce and contemporary issues.

UK RRP: £7.50

Hadīth for Beginners
A concise Hadīth book with various Ahādeeth that relate to basic Ibādāh and moral etiquettes in Islām accessible to a wider readership. Each Hadīth has been presented with the Arabic text, its translation and commentary to enlighten the reader, its meaning and application in day-to-day life.

UK RRP: £3.00

Du'ā for Beginners
This book contains basic Du'ās which every Muslim should recite on a daily basis. Highly recommended to young children and adults studying at Islamic schools and Madrasahs so that one may cherish the beautiful treasure of supplications of our beloved Prophet ﷺ in one's daily life, which will ultimately bring peace and happiness in both worlds, Inshā-Allāh.

UK RRP: £2.00

How well do you know Islām?
An exciting educational book which contains 300 multiple questions and answers to help you increase your knowledge on Islām! Ideal for the whole family, especially children and adult students to learn new knowledge in an enjoyable way and cherish the treasures of knowledge that you will acquire from this book. A very beneficial tool for educational syllabus.

UK RRP: £3.00

Treasures of the Holy Qur'ān
This book entitled "Treasures of the Holy Qur'ān" has been compiled to create a stronger bond between the Holy Qur'ān and the readers. It mentions the different virtues of Sūrahs and verses from the Holy Qur'ān with the hope that the readers will increase their zeal and enthusiasm to recite and inculcate the teachings of the Holy Qur'ān into their daily lives.

UK RRP: £3.00

Other titles from JKN PUBLICATIONS

Marriage - A Complete Solution
Islām regards marriage as a great act of worship. This book has been designed to provide the fundamental teachings and guidelines of all what relates to the marital life in a simplified English language. It encapsulates in a nutshell all the marriage laws mentioned in many of the main reference books in order to facilitate their understanding and implementation.

UK RRP: £5.00

Pearls of Luqmān
This book is a comprehensive commentary of Sūrah Luqmān, written beautifully by Shaykh Mufti Saiful Islām. It offers the reader with an enquiring mind, abundance of advice, guidance, counselling and wisdom.

The reader will be enlightened by many wonderful topics and anecdotes mentioned in this book, which will create a greater understanding of the Holy Qur'ān and its wisdom. The book highlights some of the wise sayings and words of advice Luqmān ﷺ gave to his son.

UK RRP: £3.00

Arabic Grammar Beginners
This book is a study of Arabic Grammar based on the subject of Nahw (Syntax) in a simplified English format. If a student studies this book thoroughly, he/she will develop a very good foundation in this field, Inshā-Allāh. Many books have been written on this subject in various languages such as Arabic, Persian and Urdu. However, in this day and age there is a growing demand for this subject to be available in English.

UK RRP: £3.00

A Gift to My Youngsters
This treasure filled book, is a collection of Islamic stories, morals and anecdotes from the life of our beloved Prophet ﷺ, his Companions ﷺ and the pious predecessors. The stories and anecdotes are based on moral and ethical values, which the reader will enjoy sharing with their peers, friends, families and loved ones.

"A Gift to My Youngsters" – is a wonderful gift presented to the readers personally, by the author himself, especially with the youngsters in mind. He has carefully selected stories and anecdotes containing beautiful morals, lessons and valuable knowledge and wisdom.

UK RRP: £5.00

Travel Companion

The beauty of this book is that it enables a person on any journey, small or distant or simply at home, to utilise their spare time to read and benefit from an exciting and vast collection of important and interesting Islamic topics and lessons. Written in simple and easy to read text, this book will immensely benefit both the newly interested person in Islām and the inquiring mind of a student expanding upon their existing knowledge. Inspiring reminders from the Holy Qur'ān and the blessed words of our beloved Prophet ﷺ beautifies each topic and will illuminate the heart of the reader.

UK RRP: £5.00

Pearls of Wisdom

Junaid Baghdādi ﷺ once said, "Allāh ﷻ strengthens through these Islamic stories the hearts of His friends, as proven from the Qur'anic verse,
"And all that We narrate unto you of the stories of the Messengers, so as to strengthen through it your heart." (11:120)
Mālik Ibn Dinār ﷺ stated that such stories are gifts from Paradise. He also emphasised to narrate these stories as much as possible as they are gems and it is possible that an individual might find a truly rare and invaluable gem among them.

UK RRP: £6.00

Inspirations

This book contains a compilation of selected speeches delivered by Shaykh Mufti Saiful Islām on a variety of topics such as the Holy Qur'ān, Nikāh and eating Halāl. Having previously been compiled in separate booklets, it was decided that the transcripts be gathered together in one book for the benefit of the reader. In addition to this, we have included in this book, further speeches which have not yet been printed.

UK RRP: £6.00

Gift to my Sisters

A thought provoking compilation of very interesting articles including real life stories of pious predecessors, imaginative illustrations and much more. All designed to influence and motivate mothers, sisters, wives and daughters towards an ideal Islamic lifestyle. A lifestyle referred to by our Creator, Allāh ﷻ in the Holy Qur'ān as the means to salvation and ultimate success.

UK RRP: £6.00

Gift to my Brothers

A thought provoking compilation of very interesting articles including real life stories of pious predecessors, imaginative illustrations, medical advices on intoxicants and rehabilitation and much more. All designed to influence and motivate fathers, brothers, husbands and sons towards an ideal Islamic lifestyle. A lifestyle referred to by our Creator, Allāh ﷻ in the Holy Qur'ān as the means to salvation and ultimate success.

UK RRP: £5.00

Heroes of Islām
"In the narratives there is certainly a lesson for people of intelligence (understanding)." (12:111)

A fine blend of Islamic personalities who have been recognised for leaving a lasting mark in the hearts and minds of people.

A distinguishing feature of this book is that the author has selected not only some of the most world and historically famous renowned scholars but also these lesser known and a few who have simply left behind a valuable piece of advice to their nearest and dearest. **UK RRP: £5.00**

Ask a Mufti (3 volumes)

Muslims in every generation have confronted different kinds of challenges. Inspite of that, Islām produced such luminary Ulamā who confronted and responded to the challenges of their time to guide the Ummah to the straight path. "Ask A Mufti" is a comprehensive three volume fatwa book, based on the Hanafi School, covering a wide range of topics related to every aspect of human life such as belief, ritual worship, life after death and contemporary legal topics related to purity, commercial transaction, marriage, divorce, food, cosmetic, laws pertaining to women, Islamic medical ethics and much more.

UK RRP: £30.00

Should I Follow a Madhab?

Taqleed or following one of the four legal schools is not a new phenomenon. Historically, scholars of great calibre and luminaries, each one being a specialist in his own right, were known to have adhered to one of the four legal schools. It is only in the previous century that a minority group emerged advocating a severe ban on following one of the four major schools.

This book endeavours to address the topic of Taqleed and elucidates its importance and necessity in this day and age. It will also, by the Divine Will of Allāh ﷻ dispel some of the confusion surrounding this topic. **UK RRP: £5.00**

Advice for the Students of Knowledge

Allāh ﷻ describes divine knowledge in the Holy Qur'ān as a 'Light'. Amongst the qualities of light are purity and guidance. The Holy Prophet ﷺ has clearly explained this concept in many blessed Ahādeeth and has also taught us many supplications in which we ask for beneficial knowledge.

This book is a golden tool for every sincere student of knowledge wishing to mould his/her character and engrain those correct qualities in order to be worthy of receiving the great gift of Ilm from Allāh ﷻ. **UK RRP: £3.00**

Stories for Children

"Stories for Children" - is a wonderful gift presented to the readers personally by the author himself, especially with the young children in mind. The stories are based on moral and ethical values, which the reader will enjoy sharing with their peers, friends, families and loved ones. The aim is to present to the children stories and incidents which contain moral lessons, in order to reform and correct their lives, according to the Holy Qur'ān and Sunnah.

UK RRP: £5.00

Pearls from My Shaykh
This book contains a collection of pearls and inspirational accounts of the Holy Prophet ﷺ, his noble Companions, pious predecessors and some personal accounts and sayings of our well-known contemporary scholar and spiritual guide, Shaykh Mufti Saiful Islām Sāhib. Each anecdote and narrative of the pious predecessors have been written in the way that was narrated by Mufti Saiful Islām Sāhib in his discourses, drawing the specific lessons he intended from telling the story. The accounts from the life of the Shaykh has been compiled by a particular student based on their own experience and personal observation. **UK RRP: £5.00**

Paradise & Hell
This book is a collection of detailed explanation of Paradise and Hell including the state and conditions of its inhabitants. All the details have been taken from various reliable sources. The purpose of its compilation is for the reader to contemplate and appreciate the innumerable favours, rewards, comfort and unlimited luxuries of Paradise and at the same time take heed from the punishment of Hell. Shaykh Mufti Saiful Islām Sāhib has presented this book in a unique format by including the Tafseer and virtues of Sūrah Ar-Rahmān. **UK RRP: £5.00**

Prayers for Forgiveness
Prayers for Forgiveness' is a short compilation of Du'ās in Arabic with English translation and transliteration. This book can be studied after 'Du'ā for Beginners' or as a separate book. It includes twenty more Du'ās which have not been mentioned in the previous Du'ā book. It also includes a section of Du'ās from the Holy Qur'ān and a section from the Ahādeeth. The book concludes with a section mentioning the Ninety-Nine Names of Allāh ﷻ with its translation and transliteration. **UK RRP: £3.00**

Scattered Pearls
This book is a collection of scattered pearls taken from books, magazines, emails and WhatsApp messages. These pearls will hopefully increase our knowledge, wisdom and make us realise the purpose of life. In this book, Mufti Sāhib has included messages sent to him from scholars, friends and colleagues which will be beneficial and interesting for our readers Inshā-Allāh. **UK RRP: £4.00**

Poems of Wisdom
This book is a collection of poems from those who contributed to the Al-Mumin Magazine in the poems section. The Hadeeth mentions "Indeed some form of poems are full of wisdom." The themes of each poem vary between wittiness, thought provocation, moral lessons, emotional to name but a few. The readers will benefit from this immensely and make them ponder over the outlook of life in general.
UK RRP: £4.00

Horrors of Judgement Day
This book is a detailed and informative commentary of the first three Sūrahs of the last Juz namely; Sūrah Naba, Sūrah Nāzi'āt and Sūrah Abasa. These Sūrahs vividly depict the horrific events and scenes of the Great Day in order to warn mankind the end of this world. These Sūrahs are an essential reminder for us all to instil the fear and concern of the Day of Judgement and to detach ourselves from the worldly pleasures. Reading this book allows us to attain the true realization of this world and provides essential advices of how to gain eternal salvation in the Hereafter.

RRP: £5:00

Spiritual Heart
It is necessary that Muslims always strive to better themselves at all times and to free themselves from the destructive maladies. This book focusses on three main spiritual maladies; pride, anger and evil gazes. It explains its root causes and offers some spiritual cures. Many examples from the lives of the pious predecessors are used for inspiration and encouragement for controlling the above three maladies. It is hoped that the purification process of the heart becomes easy once the underlying roots of the above maladies are clearly understood. **UK RRP: £5:00**

Hajj & Umrah for Beginners
This book is a step by step guide on Hajj and Umrah for absolute beginners. Many other additional important rulings (Masāil) have been included that will Insha-Allāh prove very useful for our readers. The book also includes some etiquettes of visiting (Ziyārat) of the Holy Prophet's ﷺ blessed Masjid and his Holy Grave.

UK RRP £3:00

Advice for the Spiritual Travellers
This book contains essential guidelines for a spiritual Murīd to gain some familiarity of the science of Tasawwuf. It explains the meaning and aims of Tasawwuf, some understanding around the concept of the soul, and general guidelines for a spiritual Murīd. This is highly recommended book and it is hoped that it gains wider readership among those Murīds who are basically new to the science of Tasawwuf.

UK RRP £3:00

Don't Worry Be Happy
This book is a compilation of sayings and earnest pieces of advice that have been gathered directly from my respected teacher Shaykh Mufti Saiful Islām Sāhib. The book consists of many valuable enlightenments including how to deal with challenges of life, promoting unity, practicing good manners, being optimistic and many other valuable advices. Our respected Shaykh has gathered this Naseehah from meditating, contemplating, analysing and searching for the gems within Qur'anic verses, Ahādeeth and teachings of our Pious Predecessors. **UK RRP £1:00**

Kanzul Bāri
Kanzul Bāri provides a detailed commentary of the Ahādeeth contained in Saheeh al-Bukhāri. The commentary includes Imām Bukhāri's ﷺ biography, the status of his book, spiritual advice, inspirational accounts along with academic discussions related to Fiqh, its application and differences of opinion. Moreover, it answers objections arising in one's mind about certain Ahādeeth. Inquisitive students of Hadeeth will find this commentary a very useful reference book in the final year of their Ālim course for gaining a deeper understanding of the science of Hadeeth. **UK RRP: £15.00**

How to Become a Friend of Allāh ﷻ
The friends of Allāh ﷻ have been described in detail in the Holy Qur'ān and Āhadeeth. This book endeavours its readers to help create a bond with Allāh ﷻ in attaining His friendship as He is the sole Creator of all material and immaterial things. It is only through Allāh's ﷻ friendship, an individual will achieve happiness in this life and the Hereafter, hence eliminate worries, sadness, depression, anxiety and misery of this world. **UK RRP:**

Gems & Jewels
This book contains a selection of articles which have been gathered for the benefit of the readers covering a variety of topics on various aspects of daily life. It offers precious advice and anecdotes that contain moral lessons. The advice captivates its readers and will extend the narrowness of their thoughts to deep reflection, wisdom and appreciation of the purpose of our existence.
UK RRP: £4.00

End of Time
This book is a comprehensive explanation of the three Sūrahs of Juzz Amma; Sūrah Takweer, Sūrah Infitār and Sūrah Mutaffifeen. This book is a continuation from the previous book of the same author, 'Horrors of Judgement Day'. The three Sūrahs vividly sketch out the scene of the Day of Judgement and describe the state of both the inmates of Jannah and Jahannam. Mufti Saiful Islām Sāhib provides an easy but comprehensive commentary of the three Sūrahs facilitating its understanding for the readers whilst capturing the horrific scene of the ending of the world and the conditions of mankind on that horrific Day. **UK RRP: £5.00**

Andalus (modern day Spain), the long lost history, was once a country that produced many great calibre of Muslim scholars comprising of Mufassirūn, Muhaddithūn, Fuqahā, judges, scientists, philosophers, surgeons, to name but a few. The Muslims conquered Andalus in 711 AD and ruled over it for eight-hundred years. This was known as the era of Muslim glory. Many non-Muslim Europeans during that time travelled to Spain to study under Muslim scholars. The remanences of the Muslim rule in Spain are manifested through their universities, magnificent palaces and Masājid carved with Arabic writings, standing even until today. In this book, Shaykh Mufti Saiful Islām shares some of his valuable experiences he witnessed during his journey to Spain. **UK RRP: £3.00**

Ideal Youth
This book contains articles gathered from various social media avenues; magazines, emails, WhatsApp and telegram messages that provide useful tips of advice for those who have the zeal to learn and consider changing their negative habits and behavior and become better Muslims to set a positive trend for the next generation. **UK RRP:£4:00**

Ideal Teacher
This book contains abundance of precious advices for the Ulamā who are in the teaching profession. It serves to present Islamic ethical principles of teaching and to remind every teacher of their moral duties towards their students. This book will Inshā-Allāh prove to be beneficial for newly graduates and scholars wanting to utilize their knowledge through teaching. **UK RRP:£4:00**

Ideal Student
This book is a guide for all students of knowledge in achieving the excellent qualities of becoming an ideal student. It contains precious advices, anecdotes of our pious predecessors and tips in developing good morals as a student. Good morals is vital for seeking knowledge. A must for all students if they want to develop their Islamic Knowledge. **UK RRP:£4:00**

Ideal Parents
This book contains a wealth of knowledge in achieving the qualities of becoming ideal parents. It contains precious advices, anecdotes of our pious predecessors and tips in developing good parenthood skills. Good morals is vital for seeking knowledge. A must for all parents . **UK RRP:£4:00**

Ideal Couple
This book is a compilation of inspiring stories and articles containing useful tips and life skills for every couple. Marriage life is a big responsibility and success in marriage is only possible if the couple know what it means to be an ideal couple. **UK RRP:£4:00**

Ideal Role Model
This book is a compilation of sayings and accounts of our pious predecessors. The purpose of this book is so we can learn from our pious predecessors the purpose of this life and how to attain closer to the Creator. Those people who inspires us attaining closeness to our Creator are our true role models. A must everyone to read. **UK RRP:£4:00**

Bangladesh– A Land of Natural Beauty
This book is a compilation of our respected Shaykh's journeys to Bangladesh including visits to famous Madāris and Masājid around the country. The Shaykh shares some of his thought provoking experiences and his personal visits with great scholars in Bangladesh. **UK RRP: £4.00**

Pearls from the Quran
This series begins with the small Sūrahs from 30th Juzz initially, unravelling its heavenly gems, precious advices and anecdotes worthy of personal reflection. It will most definitely benefit both those new to as well as advanced students of the science of Tafsīr. The purpose is to make it easily accessible for the general public in understanding the meaning of the Holy Qur'ān. **UK RRP:**